Jane Bull

Crafty
Creatures

DK

DK

LONDON, NEW YORK, MUNICH,
MELBOURNE, and DELHI

DESIGN AND TEXT Jane Bull
PHOTOGRAPHER Andy Crawford
SENIOR EDITOR Carrie Love
DESIGNER Hannah Moore

PRODUCTION EDITOR Raymond Williams
PRODUCTION CONTROLLER Ché Creasey

CREATIVE DIRECTOR Jane Bull
CATEGORY PUBLISHER Mary Ling

First published in Great Britain in 2013 by
Dorling Kindersley Limited
80 Strand, London WC2R 0RL
Penguin Group (UK)

10 9 8 7 6 5 4 3 2 1
001–185426–09/13

A CIP catalogue record for this book
is available from the British Library.

ISBN: 978-1-40932-113-2

Printed and bound in China
by South China Printing Co. Ltd.

Discover more at
www.dk.com

Meet the creatures

Creature craft

Meet a host of animal characters

The projects in this book are all simple to make – good for beginners and experienced crafters alike. All you need to get started is a basic grasp of sewing and knitting, plus the essential sewing kit. The materials required for each craft are listed at the start of each project. Happy making!

Sewing kit

See page 112

1

Woolly animals

Woolly octopus

This crazy octopus is great for practising your plaiting skills and for using up your leftover yarns – why not go for a multicoloured creature?

You will need

- 1 x colourful yarn ball • Thick card 30cm (12in) long • A ball of scrunched up foil
- Googly eyes • Scissors

The ball is slightly smaller than a tennis ball.

Give your octopus a lovely bow tie using ribbon.

How to make lots of legs

1

Wind the yarn round and round the card, about 40 times.

Secure the end of the yarn to the card.

2

Place a piece of yarn under the wound yarn at the top and tie it firmly together.

Cut through the bundle of yarn.

3

Place the centre of the bundle over the ball.

Secure the plait with a piece of yarn tied in a bow.

4

Spread the strands of yarn evenly over the ball.

Hold the ball firmly and tie a piece of yarn under the ball.

5

Divide the bundle into eight equal bunches.

Divide each bunch into three equal strands.

Plait each leg.

Knittens

These are knitted kittens — knit some stripy shapes, sew them up, add the filling until they're soft and cuddly, then add buttons for the eyes, and you have a Knitten.

You will need

- Double knit yarn for body and contrasting colours for clothes
- Knitting needles 4mm (No 6)
- Tapestry needle • Soft toy stuffing
- Buttons for eyes • Sewing kit (see page 112)

Head

Top

Sleeve

Paws

Trousers

Feet

Begin knitting from the feet upwards.

How to knit a knitten

To make the knitten's body

Cast on 34 stitches in brown yarn.
Use stocking stitch (see page 121),
Feet: Starting with a row of knit stitch
work 4 rows.
Trousers: Change yarn colour
(see page 116) and work 13 rows.
Top: Change yarn colour and
work 10 rows.
Head: Change yarn colour and work
16 rows.
Cast off.

To make the arms

Cast on 9 stitches in brown yarn.
Use stocking stitch.
Paws: Starting with a row of
knit stitch, work 4 rows.
Sleeve: Change yarn colour
and make 10 rows.
Cast off.

Knitten know-how

The secret to the knitten's shape is
how it is put together. Join the
two long sides together, turn them
right way out and make sure the
seam is moved to the centre back.
This will be where the legs are
shaped (see page 16).

Stripy top or not?

Stripes are pretty, but your
knitten's top will look just as good
in one colour and will be simpler
to make too. Even better, if you
have multicoloured yarn you'll
get a colourful
effect instantly.

---

1 Sew the two long edges together to using overstitch (see page 114).

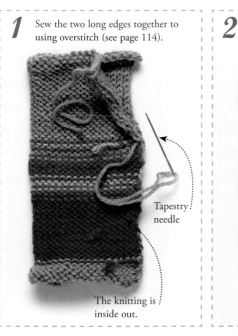

Tapestry needle

The knitting is inside out.

2 Turn right side out and move the join to the middle.

Sew along the bottom of the tube.

3 Fill the knitted pocket, but not too full.

Sew along the edge to close the opening.

4 Shaping the head

Start at the back of the head.

Use running stitch (see page 114) around the neck line.

Pull the yarn tight to gather the knitting.

Secure the yarn at the back of the head.

5 Shaping the ears and legs

To form the ear shape pinch the corner of the head.

Sew along the seam at the back of the body.

Sew at an angle to make a triangle shape.

Bring the yarn backwards and forwards through the body.

6 Adding the arms

Position the arms just below the head.

Put a small amount of stuffing in the arm.

Sew the arm together and turn the right side out.

With the arm seam facing the body, stitch the arm in position.

Cats and kittens

Cats come in all shapes and sizes. It's possible to make big and little cats by knitting different-sized rectangles. Cast on more stitches for fat cats or knit deeper stripes for tall cats.

Add buttons for the eyes.

Tops and trousers

The bands of knitted colour will become the Knitten's clothes. The bands can be plain, or try giving them stripy jumpers like the ones shown here.

Large-sized Knitten

Baby-sized Knitten

Multicolour

If you use multicoloured yarn, you can get a variety of colours without having to change yarns.

Hey there!
Use balls of different coloured
double-knit wools to make me
and my friends.

Koala   Koala Kid   Grey Bear   Mouse   Knitten

Koala Bear and friends

It's all about the ears — that's what makes these critters different. Use the Knitten method to begin the body then knit rounded or pointed ear shapes to create your creature.

Big Knitten

The Rabbits and Polar Bear

Raccoon

How to knit koalas...

These creatures are made in the same way as the Knitten on page 14. Make rectangular shapes for the arms and body with different stripes to represent the head, body, and paws. The ears are what makes them look different.

To make a round head shape gather up the knitting at the top

The neck has been gathered on this stripe to give his jumper a high neckline.

Koala Kid

FOR BODY
Cast on 24 stitches.
Work in stocking stitch.
Legs 10 rows.
Body 18 rows.
Head 15 rows.

FOR ARMS
Cast on 8 stitches.
Work in stocking stitch.
Paws 4 rows.
Arms 12 rows.

FOR EARS
Cast on 8 stitches.
Work 5 rows in stocking stitch.
Attach as shown opposite.

Koala Bear

FOR BODY
Cast on 48 stitches.
Work in stocking stitch.
Legs 20 rows.
Body 36 rows.
Head 30 rows.

FOR ARMS
Cast on 16 stitches.
Work in stocking stitch.
Paws 8 rows.
Arms 24 rows.

FOR EARS
Cast on 16 stitches.
Work 10 rows in stocking stitch.
Attach as shown opposite.

...and friends

The rabbits
Ears: Cast on 6.
Work 14 rows.

Raccoon
Ears: Cast on 4.
Work 5 rows.

Polar bear
Ears: Cast on 4.
Work 5 rows.
Work in stripes
as Koala.

Mouse
See opposite.

Grey bear
Ears: Cast on 6.
Work 6 rows.

Work in multicoloured stripes. Work as Koala.

Legs: work 11 rows. Body: work 14 rows. Head: work 15 rows. Arms: 12 rows for arm, 4 rows for sleeve.

Legs: work 6 rows.
Body: work 10 rows for trousers, 8 rows for top. Head: work 15 rows. Arms as Koala.

Legs: work 6 rows. Body: work 18 rows (work in two coloured stripes).
Head: work 8 rows grey yarn, 3 rows black yarn, 5 rows grey yarn. Arms as Koala.

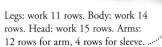

Making faces

Place a disc of white fabric on the reverse side of the head. Stitch the features in place. ....

MOUSE
Ears: Cast on 6.
Work 6 rows.

Legs: 6 rows.
Body: 11 rows for trousers, 9 rows for top.
Head: 18 rows.

Stitch from the front to position the features correctly.

Make the toy as Knitten on pages 15–16.

For a rounded head effect gather the top of the head.

Continue to sew the edges together.

Making ears

1 Cast on 8 stitches.

Work 6 rows in stocking stitch.

2 Cut the yarn, thread it on to a needle, and collect up the stitches.

3 Pull the threaded needle all the way through the loops.

Pull the yarn tight to gather the loops.

To stop the gather from loosening, sew the yarn back and forth to secure.

Thread the .... loose end on to a needle.

Use the loose end to stitch the ear to the head. .

For Li'l Ted
You will need

- 1 x ball double knit yarn in brown • Size 2.75mm (No 2) knitting needles • Soft toy stuffing
- Buttons for eyes and nose
- Sewing kit (see page 112)

How tall are the Teds?

Little Ted stands 18cm (7in) high and Big Ted is 33cm (13in) tall.

Follow me Li'l Ted, bend and stretch.

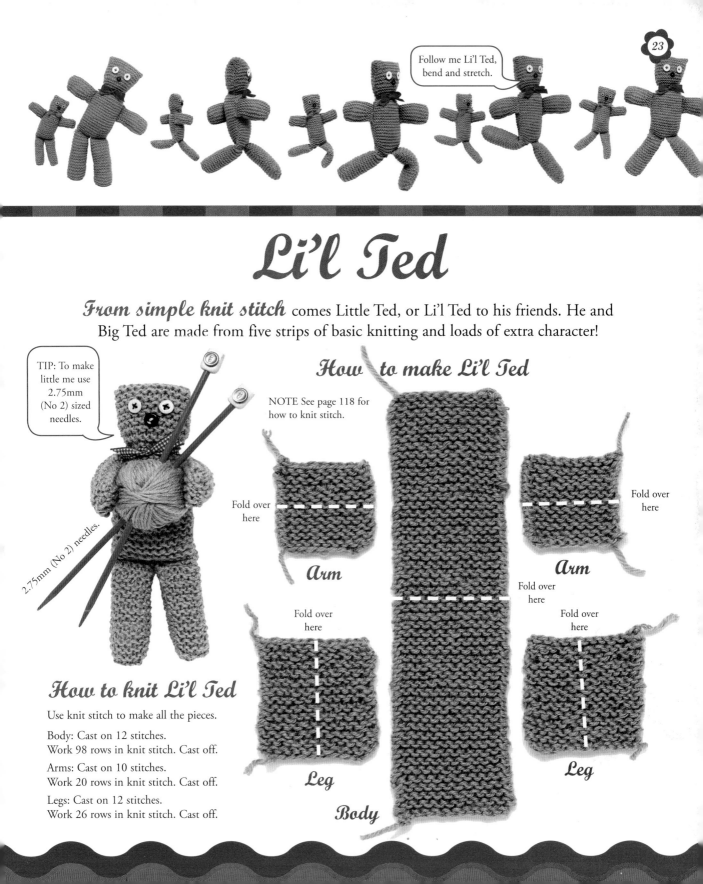

Li'l Ted

From simple knit stitch comes Little Ted, or Li'l Ted to his friends. He and Big Ted are made from five strips of basic knitting and loads of extra character!

TIP: To make little me use 2.75mm (No 2) sized needles.

2.75mm (No 2) needles.

How to make Li'l Ted

NOTE See page 118 for how to knit stitch.

Fold over here

Arm

Fold over here

Arm

Fold over here

Leg

Fold over here

Fold over here

Leg

Body

How to knit Li'l Ted

Use knit stitch to make all the pieces.

Body: Cast on 12 stitches.
Work 98 rows in knit stitch. Cast off.

Arms: Cast on 10 stitches.
Work 20 rows in knit stitch. Cast off.

Legs: Cast on 12 stitches.
Work 26 rows in knit stitch. Cast off.

Keep up Li'l Ted, run, step, and jump.

1

Using a tapestry needle, stitch up the sides leaving one end open.

Fold the pieces in half as shown on the previous page.

Neatly sew using overstitch (see page 114).

2

Turn all the pieces inside out.

Fill all the pieces with soft toy stuffing – but not too full. Ted has to move his arms and legs.

3

Neatly sew using overstitch (see page 114).

Attach the arms about a third of the way down the body.

Attach the legs from the corners of the body.

4

With a sewing needle and thread, sew on his eyes and nose.

Tie a ribbon around the body above the arms to make a head and neck.

Steady Li'l Ted, don't go crazy...

Ta daaaaa!

For Big Ted you will need

- Size 4mm (No 6) knitting needles
- Other materials as for Li'l Ted on page 22

How to knit Big Ted

Use knit stitch to make all the pieces.
Body: Cast on 20 stitches. Work 136 rows in knit stitch. Cast off.
Arms: Cast on 15 stitches. Work 32 rows in knit stitch. Cast off.
Legs: Cast on 20 stitches. Work 40 rows in knit stitch. Cast off.

Ted ideas

Use other colours of wool to make Ted. He can be blue or green or even pink! Why not try a multicoloured Ted, either with self-coloured yarn or made from all your leftover yarn.

Odd bods

Pair up your odd gloves to create these curious creatures. These three look like they're snug and warm, as if they're each wearing a jumper.

1 Turn the gloves inside out, cut the middle fingers and thumbs off. Stitch the finger and thumb holes to close them up.

2 Fill up the ears or leave them floppy.

Fill all the pieces to make the head, body, arms, and tail.

3 Attach the head to the body: tuck one glove into the top of the other glove and pin in position.

Stitch on the arms and tail.

4 Sew on the buttons for eyes.

Stitch on the felt nose and embroider the mouth.

TOP TIP If the head glove is too long – cut some of the cuff off to make a better fit.

For the ears, leave them as they are or fold them over and hold down with a couple of stitches.

A box of monkeys

Kick off your old socks and bring a sock monkey to life. See those socks transform into a cheeky monkey – the smaller the socks the cuter the monkey will be.

See here how two socks can be divided up to make one sock monkey.

Arms x 2

Nose

Ear

Tail

Ear

Body and Legs

=

You will need

• Socks • Sewing kit (see page 112) • Soft toy stuffing • Buttons for eyes

Large or small socks?

Have fun using old or new socks to make your monkeys. Try tiny socks for babies, small socks for children, and big ones for adults.

How to make a monkey

Body and legs

1

Turn the socks inside out and lay them flat with the heel facing forward.

Use backstitch (see page 114) to stitch from the heel down and around as shown.

Cut along the centre of the stitching to form the legs.

Tail, arms, nose, and ears

2

Cut out the body pieces as shown on page 28.

Join the sides by stitching along the edges using overstitch (page 114), leaving openings for stuffing.

Sew in a semicircle for the ears.

Ready to fill

3

Turn all the body pieces right side out, then fill them.

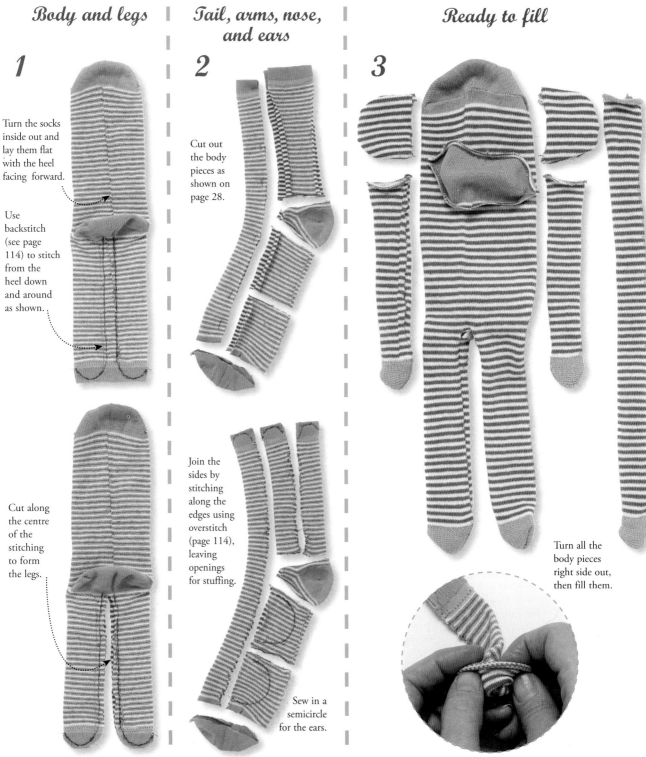

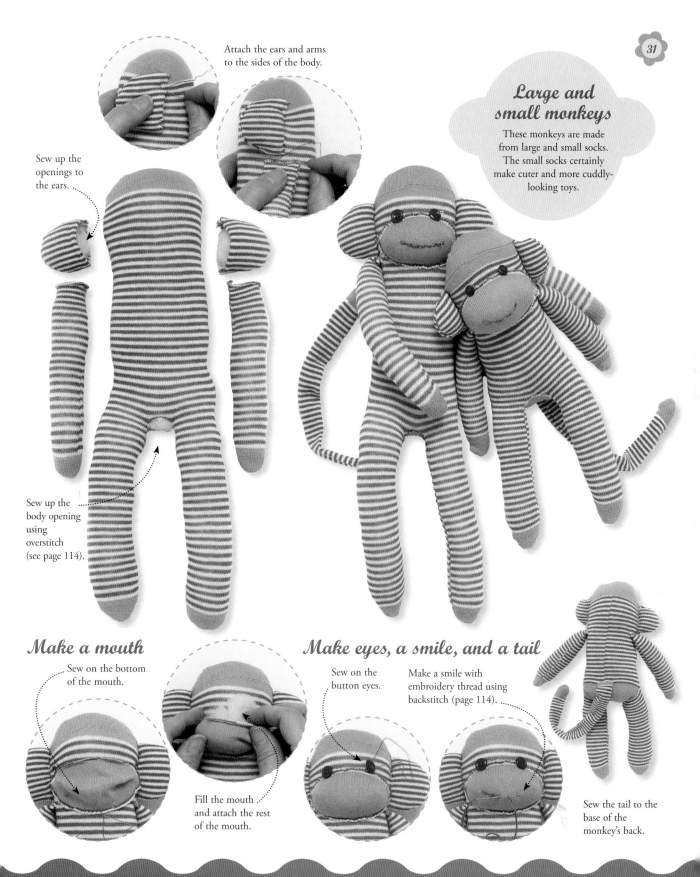

Attach the ears and arms to the sides of the body.

Sew up the openings to the ears.

Large and small monkeys

These monkeys are made from large and small socks. The small socks certainly make cuter and more cuddly-looking toys.

Sew up the body opening using overstitch (see page 114).

Make a mouth

Sew on the bottom of the mouth.

Fill the mouth and attach the rest of the mouth.

Make eyes, a smile, and a tail

Sew on the button eyes.

Make a smile with embroidery thread using backstitch (page 114).

Sew the tail to the base of the monkey's back.

Ducklings

These ducks lay eggs with a suprise inside. The simple knitted shapes hide their secrets in their plump curves. A knitted ribbed edge keeps each secret safe inside.

You will need

- Small balls of double-knit yarn
- Knitting needles 4mm (No 6)
- Sewing kit (see page 112)
- Soft toy stuffing
- Beads for eyes
- Felt for the beak

How to knit the duck's body

Shape the body

Cast on 22 stitches.
Rows 1–3 Knit 1, purl 1 (stocking stitch) to the end of each row.
Row 4 Knit 1, make 1, then knit to the end (23 stitches).
Rows 5–18 Work as Row 4, continuing to add a stitch to each row (up to 36 stitches).

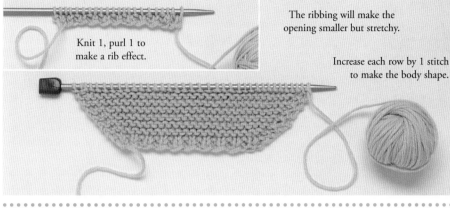

Knit 1, purl 1 to make a rib effect.

The ribbing will make the opening smaller but stretchy.

Increase each row by 1 stitch to make the body shape.

Shape the tail

Row 1 Knit 4, bring the yarn forward, turn the work round.
Row 2 Knit 4 to the end.
Row 3 Knit 3, bring the yarn forward, turn the work round.
Row 4 Knit 3 to the end.
Row 5 Knit 2, bring the yarn forward, turn the work round.
Row 6 Knit 2 to the end.
Row 7 Cast off 10 stitches and knit to the end (26 stitches remain).
Repeat from Row 1 – ending with 16 stitches remaining

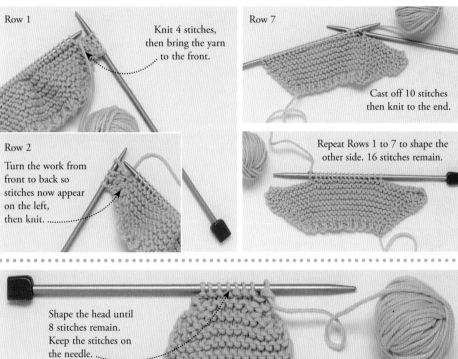

Row 1

Knit 4 stitches, then bring the yarn to the front.

Row 2

Turn the work from front to back so stitches now appear on the left, then knit.

Row 7

Cast off 10 stitches then knit to the end.

Repeat Rows 1 to 7 to shape the other side. 16 stitches remain.

Shape the head

Rows 1–5 Work in knit stitch to the end of each row.
Row 6 Knit 1, knit 2 together, then knit to the last 3 stitches. Knit 2 together, knit 1 at the end.
Rows 7, 8, and 9 Continue decreasing as for Row 6 (8 stitches remain).
Rows 10 and 11 Work in knit stitch to the end of each row.

Shape the head until 8 stitches remain. Keep the stitches on the needle.

How to make the duck's body

1 Cut the yarn leaving a 15cm (6in) length.

...Thread an embroidery needle and pick up the stitches from the knitting needle.

2 Collect up all the stitches and pull the thread all the way through the loops.

3 ...Pull the yarn tight to gather up the knitting.

Sew in this loose end as well.

Sew along the edge to join the two sides together.

4 Fill the head area only.

Put in a small amount of filling.

5 Adjust the filling to make a head and neck shape.

Place the surprise gift inside the duck.

6 Beads for eyes

Adjust the knitting to make a good duck shape with a perky tail.

Cut out the felt beak shape.

7 Sew the beak in place.

Sew on the beady eyes and shape the beak.

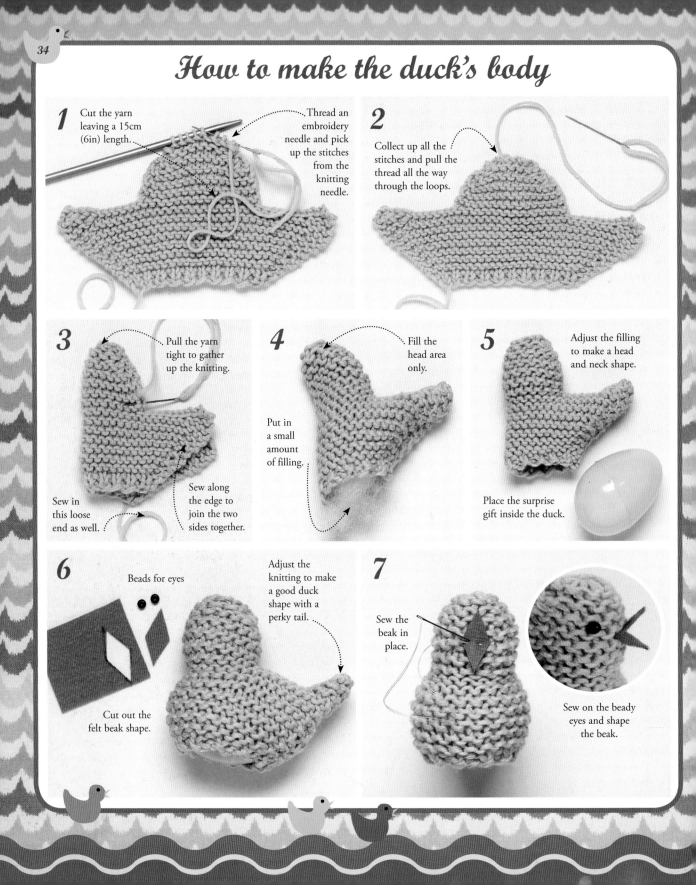

Full of surprises

These plastic egg-shaped containers are just right for small gifts, and fit perfectly inside the ducks. Alternatively, wrap up a small parcel to tuck inside.

2

Friends in felt

Pocket pets

Rover

These little critters are all made using the same basic template design. Just change ears, beaks, and snouts to create all kinds of different pals.

Basic body shape for all the pets.

Trace over the shapes to make a paper pattern. Turn to page 40 to see how.

Pinky the Pig comes to visit

How to make Rover's house

Take a large juice carton, cut it down to make a cube shape and cut out a door. Cover the sides and roof with felt.

Sit the house on a grassy felt mat.

Cut a strip of green felt with a spiky edge to create flower stalks.

Ribbit

Pinky

Cheeky

Patch

Li'l Chick

You will need

- Coloured felt – 10cm x 8cm
  (4in x 3¼in) for each body
- Felt scraps for noses and eyes
- Sewing kit (see page 112)
- Soft toy stuffing

Rover

Red

Kitty

Tie a key ring to a length of ribbon, and stitch the ribbon to the head of the pet.

Stitch a safety pin to the back to make a brooch.

Working pets

Keep your pets as little creatures in your pockets or turn them into something. Use them as fobs for your keys or hang them on a bag. Alternatively, sew a pin to the back and have your pet as a brooch.

How to make a paper pattern

Place tracing paper over the picture on the page. Trace over each of the features separately – the basic body shape, the ears, and any other features. Cut these out and pin them to the felt. Use this method to make your big pet too.

Trace over the basic body shape, then the ears, patch, and collar.

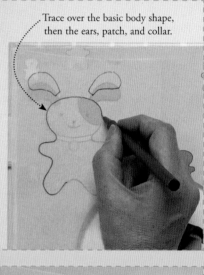

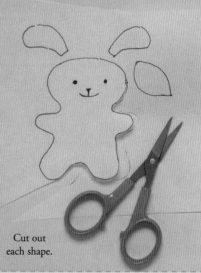

Cut out each shape.

Use this method to make the body shape for the other pets.

How to make Rover

Use this method to make all the pets. It's easier to stitch the face and the
nose on the front piece first before attaching it to the back shape.

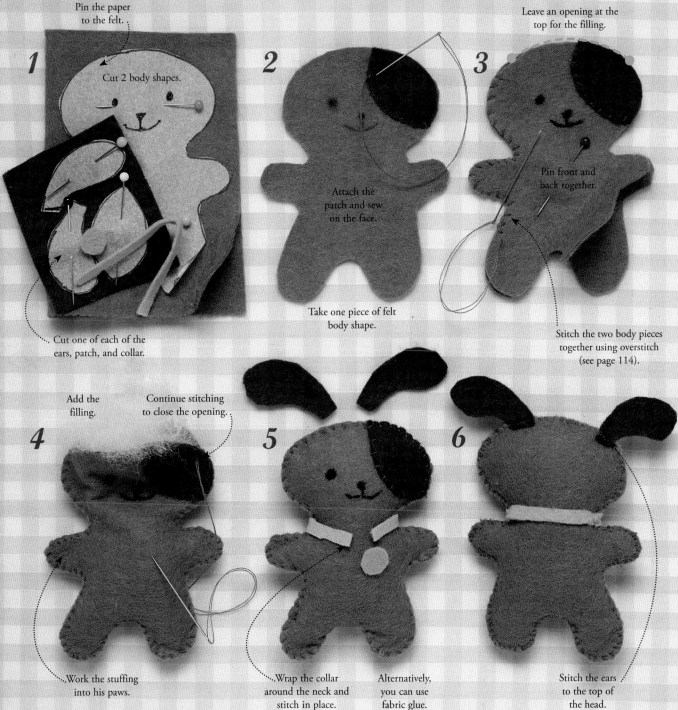

1

Pin the paper
to the felt.

Cut 2 body shapes.

Cut one of each of the
ears, patch, and collar.

2

Attach the
patch and sew
on the face.

Take one piece of felt
body shape.

3

Leave an opening at the
top for the filling.

Pin front and
back together.

Stitch the two body pieces
together using overstitch
(see page 114).

4

Add the
filling.

Work the stuffing
into his paws.

5

Continue stitching
to close the opening.

Wrap the collar
around the neck and
stitch in place.

Alternatively,
you can use
fabric glue.

6

Stitch the ears
to the top of
the head.

Make a large Rover

You can also make larger versions
of all your pets.

Trace over the
template shown here
and follow the steps
used for making the
little pet.

Use this template to
make large versions
of all your pets.

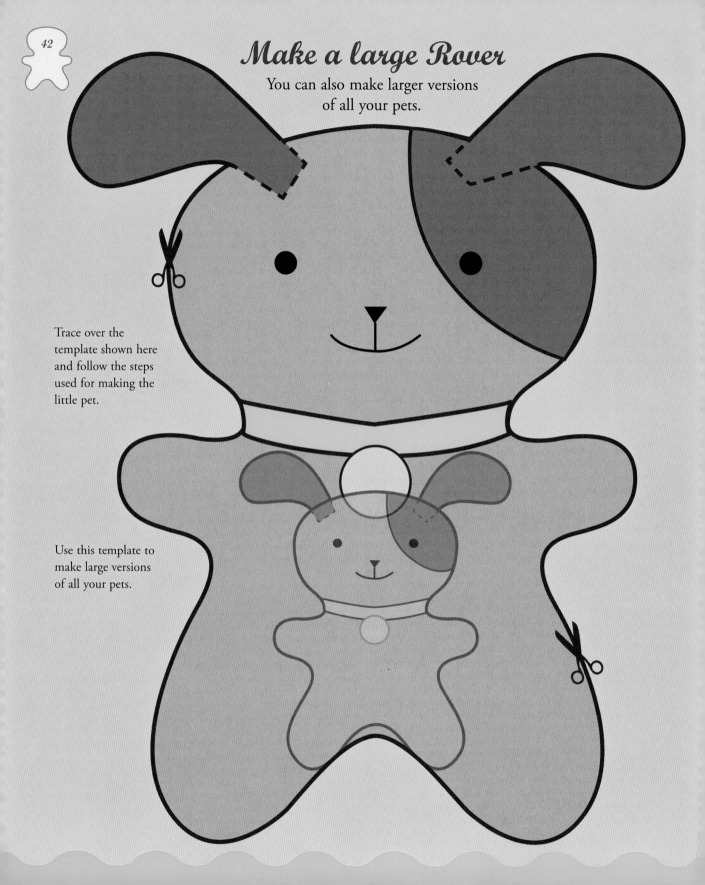

To make the ears stand up better, use two pieces of felt stitched together.

Little and Large Rover

Large pets make great cuddly soft toys. Trace the template opposite, then make it by following the steps for making the little pet.

Place the sling straps around the large pet's neck and stitch the ends of the straps together.

Cut lengths of felt 15cm x 1cm (6in x ½in) for the straps.

Make a sling

Cut a piece of felt 6cm x 9½cm (2½in x 3¾in), fold over the lower edge, and stitch up the side using overstitch.

Check that the size of the felt sling is big enough for your pet to fit in easily, you may need to adjust the dimensions slightly.

Big pets

How to make bags

Cut out a piece of felt larger than the size of the pet. Shape the felt and sew the sides together. Finally sew on the felt straps. See page 42 for more about sizes.

Match up your pocket pets to their bigger friends.

Tip

To make the ears and eyes stand up straight, double the thickness of the felt and stitch the edges together.

Cut a zig-zag edge for a broken shell effect.

Add a felt stalk and leaf.

Big Chick
with L'il Chick in an egg-shaped bag.

Big Pinky
with Pinky in an apple-shaped bag.

Each little pet has its own carry bag, just right for them.

How to make big pets

Follow the instructions on the previous pages. Enlarge the basic large pet template, draw paper templates for the ears, eyes, and other features. Sew the felt pieces together as shown for the small pocket pet on page 41.

Cut the felt into a lily pad leaf shape.

Add a felt lily to finish off the bag.

Use running stitch for the veins of the leaf.

Back stitch the whiskers and eyelashes.

A plain bag as used for the small Rover pet.

Big Ribbit
with Ribbit in a lily pad-shaped bag.

Big Blue Cat
with Blue Cat in a cat mat-shaped bag.

Mobile owls

Twirling and twisting — these mobiles work just as well on their own or in a group. Each owl is self-contained in its hoop.

You will need

- Felt for body a little smaller than embroidery hoop • Scraps of colourful felt for wings, feet, and face • Sewing kit (see page 112) • Soft toy stuffing • Buttons for eyes • Length of cotton fabric or ribbon (1¼ yards) • Wooden embroidery hoop 14cm (5½in) • Ribbon for hanging up

Owl template

Trace over the shapes to make a paper pattern. Turn to page 40 to see how this is done.

How to make an Owl

Prepare all the felt pieces using the template on page 46.

1 Take one body piece of felt and attach the features using overstitch (see page 114).

2 On the reverse, attach the wings and the feet.

Make the stitches neat and small.

3 Sew the front and back body pieces together.

Leave an opening at the base.

4 Fill the owl shape from the base and stitch shut

5 Take a strip of patterned fabric 3cm (1in) wide and wrap it around the hoop. Hold it in place with a few stitches.

Wooden embroidery hoop.

6 Attach the owl by sewing a length of thread to the head, and sew the other end to the fabric on the hoop.

The owl should swing freely in the hoop.

Tie a length of ribbon to the hoop and hang up the mobile.

Cosy cats

Here are a couple of contented cats — their simple quirky shape and flat base help them to sit quite happily together.

Little cat

Cat body

Trace over the shape to make a paper pattern.

Cat base

1

Pin the two felt shapes together.

Sew the shapes together with overstitch (see page 114), leaving the bottom open.

2

Fill the cat shape from the base.

Pin the base to the body and overstitch in place.

3

Add buttons for the eyes and pink felt for the ears.

Sew on the features to finish off your cat.

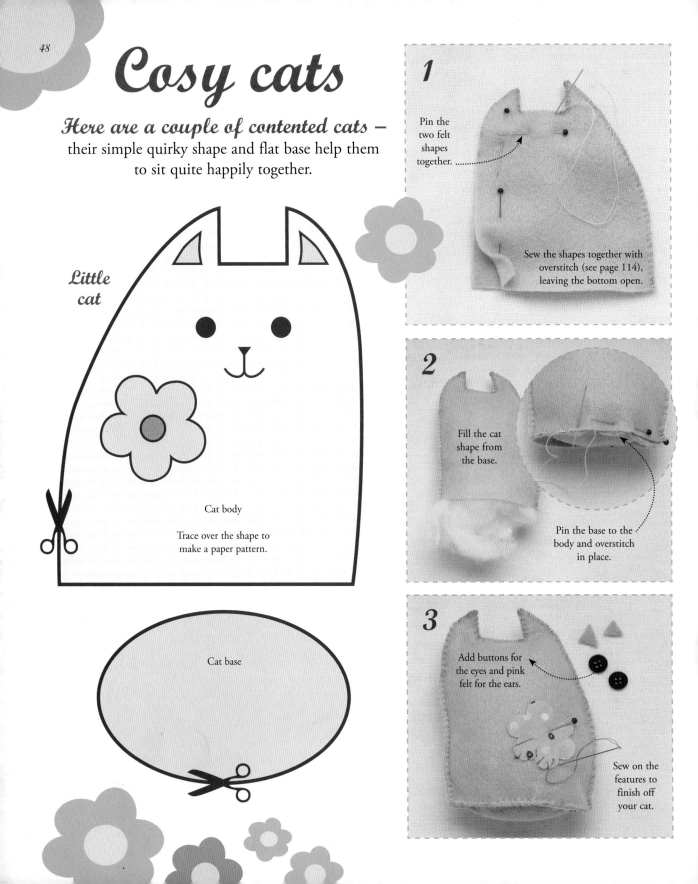

Bigger cats

To make a bigger cat simply enlarge the template on a photocopier, cut out the shapes and use the copies as your paper pattern. This big cat was made by increasing the template by 200 per cent.

You will need

Cut 2 felt shapes for the body 13cm x 12cm (5¼in x 4¾in).

Sewing kit (see page 112), buttons for eyes, felt ears, fabric motif, and sewing thread.

Cut one felt shape for the base 10cm x 6cm (3½in x 2½in).

Spring chickens

Make flocks of colourful birds. This busy clutch of chicks made from colourful scraps of felt. Their wire legs give each one its own individual character.

You will need
- Colourful felt • 1m (3ft) plastic covered wire • Soft toy stuffing
- Embroidery thread
- Sewing kit (see page 112)

How to make a chick

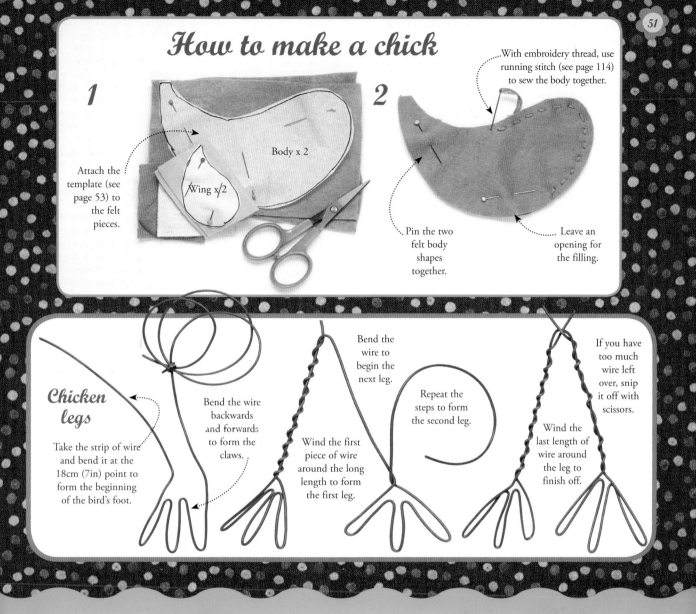

1

Attach the template (see page 53) to the felt pieces.

Body x 2

Wing x 2

2

With embroidery thread, use running stitch (see page 114) to sew the body together.

Pin the two felt body shapes together.

Leave an opening for the filling.

Chicken legs

Take the strip of wire and bend it at the 18cm (7in) point to form the beginning of the bird's foot.

Bend the wire backwards and forwards to form the claws.

Wind the first piece of wire around the long length to form the first leg.

Bend the wire to begin the next leg.

Repeat the steps to form the second leg.

If you have too much wire left over, snip it off with scissors.

Wind the last length of wire around the leg to finish off.

cheep cheep

3

Fill the bird until it feels soft, but still a little firm.

After positioning the legs (see below), add more filling to puff out the stomach more.

4

With embroidery thread, use running stitch (see page 114) to sew on the wing.

Continue to sew on the features on each side.

Push the legs into the filling as far as they will go. Hold the legs firmly between your fingers and thumb.

Sew up the opening, stitching tightly around the legs.

Bend the feet at the ankle.

Adjust the angle of the feet so the bird stands up.

chirp chirp

Get the chicken shape

The simple body shape is echoed in the wings, and finished off with a beady eye and triangular beak. Try using lots of contrasting colours.

Mice made easy

Cut out a disc of pretty cotton fabric. By simply folding it in half you can create a charming little mouse shape.

Any lightweight cotton or felt fabric will work.

Cut a disc of fabric 11cm (4¼in) wide.

You will need
- Cotton fabric for body 13cm x 13cm (5¼in x 5¼in)
- Felt for ears • Beads for eyes
- Sewing kit (see page 112)
- String for a tail • Soft toy filling

Ear shapes made from felt.

Pin the fabric together.

Fold the fabric in half.

1

Sew in the ears as you go.

Sew along the edge, nearly to the end.

With embroidery thread, sew in running stitch (see page 114) from the nose end.

Fill up the mouse's body.

2

Tie a knot in the end of the string.

Place the tail in the opening and sew it in place.

3

Use sewing thread to sew on beads for the eyes.

Finish sewing and fasten off.

4

Colour mix mice

Play with the colours of fabric, felt, and thread that you use. Match them or mix them up to create some stunning clashes.

Sewing tip

When sewing on the beads for the eyes, begin by sewing one eye in place then take the needle through the fabric to the other side of the head and attach the other eye. This way the eyes will dip into the fabric.

Gift ideas

• **Brooch:** Sew a safety pin to the back of a mouse.
• **Pin cushion:** Pop in some pins and add it to a sewing kit.
• **Smelly mice:** mix some dried lavender in with the filling to make a fragrant gift!

Minimals

What do you call a tiny animal?

A Minimal! These plumped up little cushions are not much bigger than your thumb.

You will need

- Colourful scraps of felt
- Soft toy stuffing • Embroidery thread
- Sewing kit (see page 112)

Pin the template (see pages 58–59) to the felt.

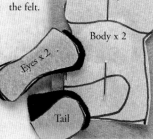

Body x 2

Eyes x 2

Tail

Decorate the front first.

Use embroidery thread to add features.

Using sewing thread, stitch the front and back together.

Fill the tiny body with a small amount of filling.

Finish off by sewing up the base.

Little boxes of Minimals

Empty matchboxes make ideal places to keep your miniature animals. Decorate the boxes with matching fabric and give them away as gifts.

Boxes of Minimals

We also make brilliant brooches.

Use these templates to create your own matchbox size Minimals. See pages 56–57.

Minimal mobiles

For a more natural effect, use twigs from the garden to hang your mini and maximals from. Sew a length of yarn to the top of the felt and tie each one to a twig.

Wild ones

Maximize your minimals to create a really wild bunch of creatures. Increase the template by 150 per cent and put them together in the same way as the tiny versions.

Bees and bugs

Swarms of bees and bugs. Get creative with felt and blanket stitch – make the cutest bees and bugs there have ever been.

You will need

- Red felt 11.5cm x 16cm (5in x 6¼in)
- Black felt 10cm x 11.5cm (3½in x 5in)
- Scraps of white felt
- Sewing kit (see page 112)
- Soft toy stuffing

Pin the templates on to the felt and cut out the shapes.

Use for body and base.

Cut out the spots and eyes.

Body

Face

Base

Trace over the bug template. Cut one base in black, two body shapes in red, six spots, and two eyes.

1

First, sew the features to the ladybird body.

2

Sew the base and one half of the body together. Use blanket stitch (see page 115).

Black base for bug.

3

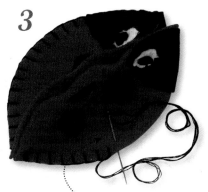

Sew the other half of the body to the base in the same way.

4

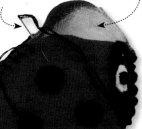

Sew the two body shapes together half way.

Add the filling.

5

Once filled, sew up the opening.

How to make bees

Cut out the body shapes, face, and eyes as for the spotty bugs. Make stripes out of black felt and two white felt wings. Sew on the strips before stitching together and add the wings at the end.

3

Sew cute

Dog's best friends

Dogs in transit. Using the fold of the fabric to make the dog's back gives these little pups a nice curvy shape. They are small enough to fit in your hand or the large ones make comfy cushions.

DOGS IN TRANSIT
handle with care

You will need

• Cotton fabric 14cm x 23cm (5½in x 9in)
• Felt scraps for ears, noses, tails, and collars
• Soft toy stuffing • Buttons for eyes • Colourful thread for mouth • Sewing kit (see page 112)

How to make friends

1

Fold fabric

Place the edge of the paper against the fold.

Fold the fabric in half with the pattern on the inside.

Pin the paper to the fabric and carefully cut around the dog shape.

2

Sew round the shape using backstitch (see page 114).

Leave an opening for the filling.

3

Turn the dog shape right side out.

Fill up the shape and carefully sew up the opening.

Slipstitch (see page 114).

Now add the features

Eyes

Nose

Ears

Collar

Tail

Stitch the ears to the top of the head.

Stitch on a mouth using backstitch (see page 114).

To attach the nose, stitch backwards and forwards through the nose fabric and felt.

Wrap the felt collar around the neck and attach in place with the button.

Attach the tail in the same way as the nose.

Find the pattern
for Dog's best friend on page 68.

Dog's best friends

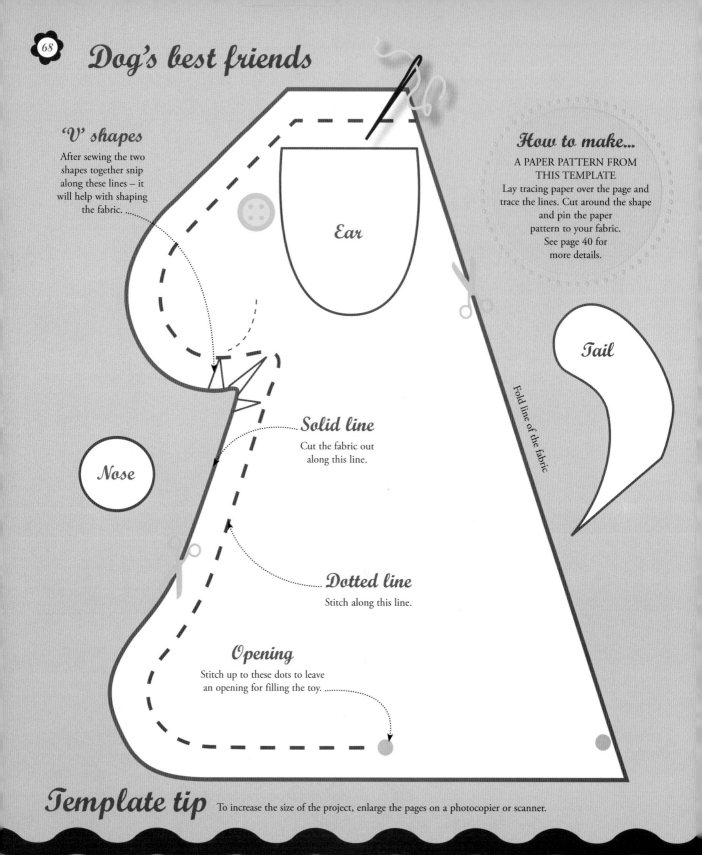

'V' shapes
After sewing the two shapes together snip along these lines – it will help with shaping the fabric.

Ear

How to make...
A PAPER PATTERN FROM THIS TEMPLATE
Lay tracing paper over the page and trace the lines. Cut around the shape and pin the paper pattern to your fabric. See page 40 for more details.

Tail

Fold line of the fabric

Solid line
Cut the fabric out along this line.

Nose

Dotted line
Stitch along this line.

Opening
Stitch up to these dots to leave an opening for filling the toy.

Template tip
To increase the size of the project, enlarge the pages on a photocopier or scanner.

Big dog cushion

Making bigger dogs is easy: simply scan the page and increase the size of the template by 200 per cent. Use the print out for your paper pattern. Simply follow the instructions as for the small dog.

This dog is made at 200 per cent.

Pretty birdies

Collect up pieces of patterned fabric to create these cute little birds. Use embroidery stitches to give the birds features and have fun with the fabric print, following the flower shapes to create a really special effect.

You will need

Patterned cotton fabric

Buttons and ribbons

Embroidery thread

How to make a bird

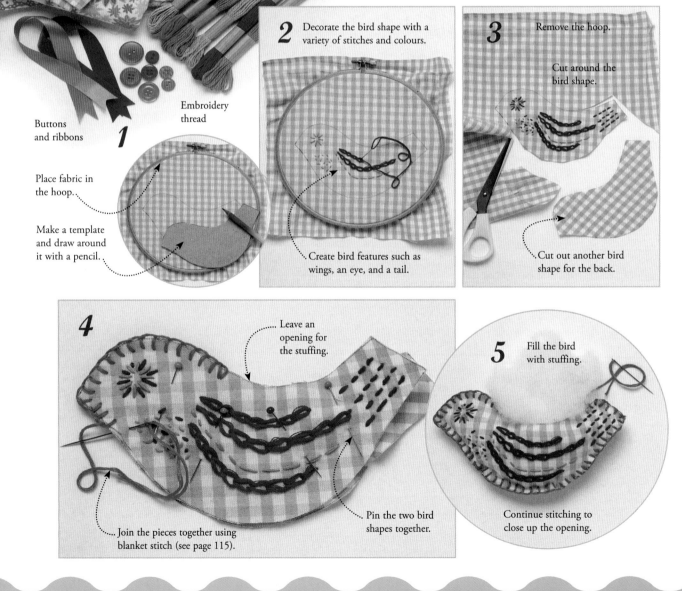

1 Place fabric in the hoop.

Make a template and draw around it with a pencil.

2 Decorate the bird shape with a variety of stitches and colours.

Create bird features such as wings, an eye, and a tail.

3 Remove the hoop.

Cut around the bird shape.

Cut out another bird shape for the back.

4 Leave an opening for the stuffing.

Pin the two bird shapes together.

Join the pieces together using blanket stitch (see page 115).

5 Fill the bird with stuffing.

Continue stitching to close up the opening.

Stitching tip

Try using the design on the patterned fabric to guide your stitches. Follow the outline of any petals, and add chain stitch leaves using threads in contrasting colours. Finish off with buttons for eyes.

Flying birds

To make hanging birds, cut a length of ribbon 20cm (8in). Fold it in half and sew it to the bird. Add a button for extra decoration.

Bunny girls

Rag-doll rabbits – here is a crafty twist on the classic rag doll. Dress these girls up and create their own fashion collection.

You will need

• Cotton fabric for each doll, 30cm x 60cm (12in x 24in) • Sewing kit (see page 112) • Soft toy filling • Patterned cotton fabric for dress, 40cm x 25cm (16in x 10in) • Felt for eyes • Rickrack and ribbon

The bunnies get together for a cup of tea

Dressed up and ready to go

- **Dresses:** Make the bunnies some pretty dresses with a matching headscarf. Decorate the dresses with strips of rickrack and ribbon.
- **Bags:** Add a matching bag to your bunny's wardrobe. Simply stitch two pieces of felt together and attach a ribbon strap.

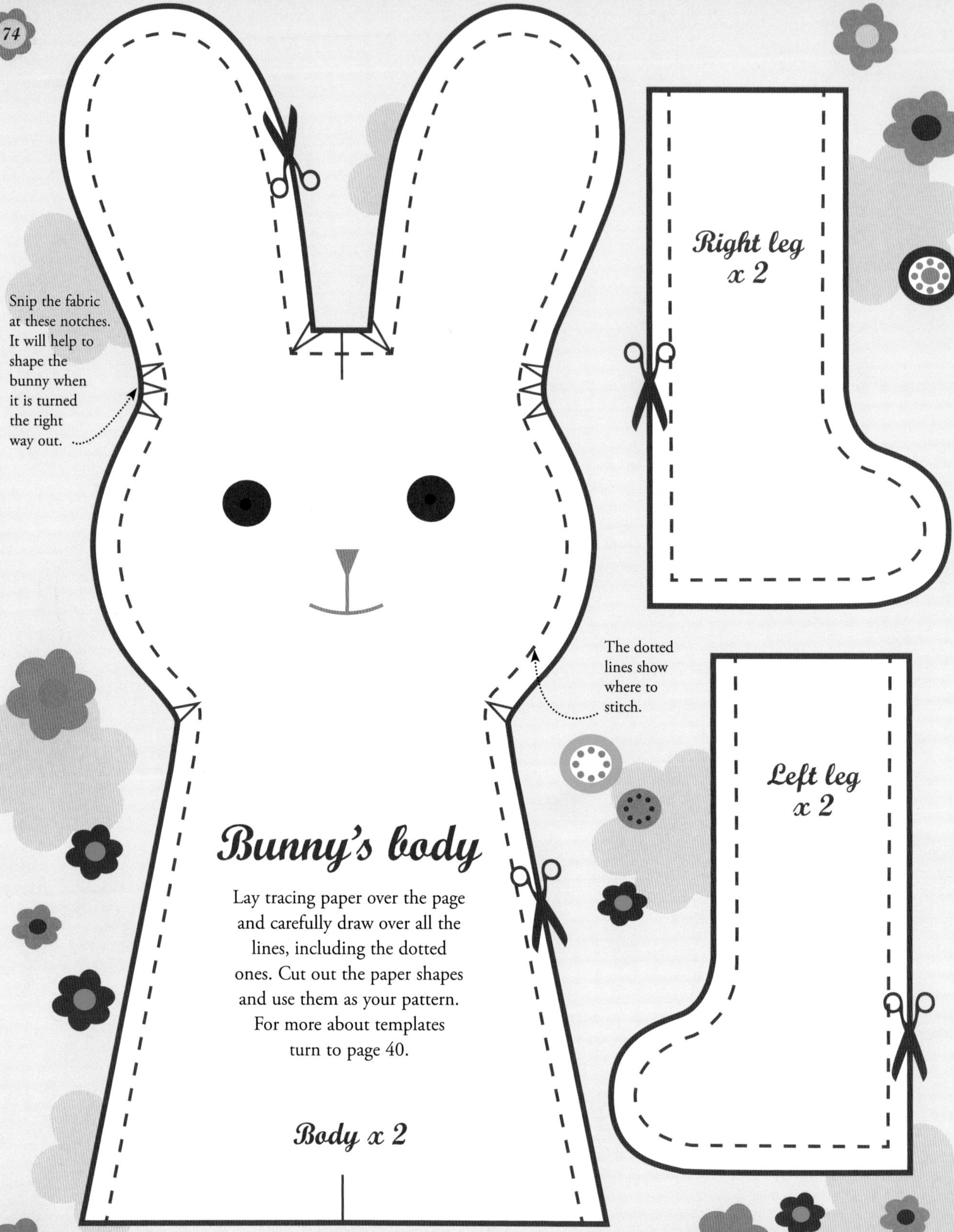

Snip the fabric at these notches. It will help to shape the bunny when it is turned the right way out.

Right leg
x 2

The dotted lines show where to stitch.

Bunny's body

Lay tracing paper over the page and carefully draw over all the lines, including the dotted ones. Cut out the paper shapes and use them as your pattern. For more about templates turn to page 40.

Left leg
x 2

Body x 2

Left arm
x 2

Bunny's bag
x 2

Like to make a bigger bunny?

If you like the idea of creating bigger bunnies, simply copy the pages and enlarge them by 25 per cent, 50 per cent, or 75 per cent. Cut out the copies and use those as your paper pattern.

Right arm
x 2

This line shows where to stitch up to, in order to leave space for the arm hole.

This dotted line is for the opening at the back of the dress. It shows how far down to cut the material.

Bunny's dress

x 2

How to make a bunny

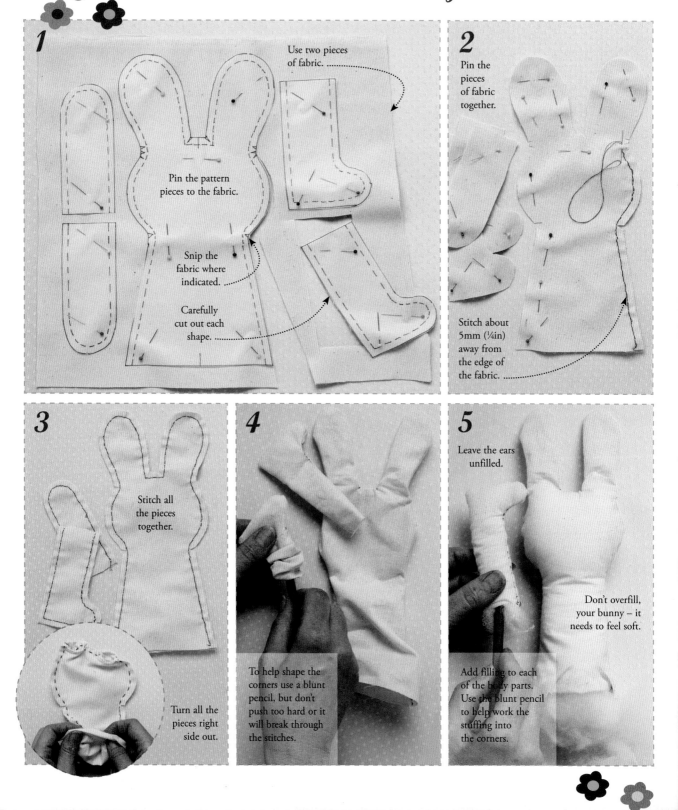

1

Use two pieces of fabric.

Pin the pattern pieces to the fabric.

Snip the fabric where indicated.

Carefully cut out each shape.

2

Pin the pieces of fabric together.

Stitch about 5mm (¼in) away from the edge of the fabric.

3

Stitch all the pieces together.

Turn all the pieces right side out.

4

To help shape the corners use a blunt pencil, but don't push too hard or it will break through the stitches.

5

Leave the ears unfilled.

Don't overfill, your bunny – it needs to feel soft.

Add filling to each of the body parts. Use the blunt pencil to help work the stuffing into the corners.

Putting bunny together

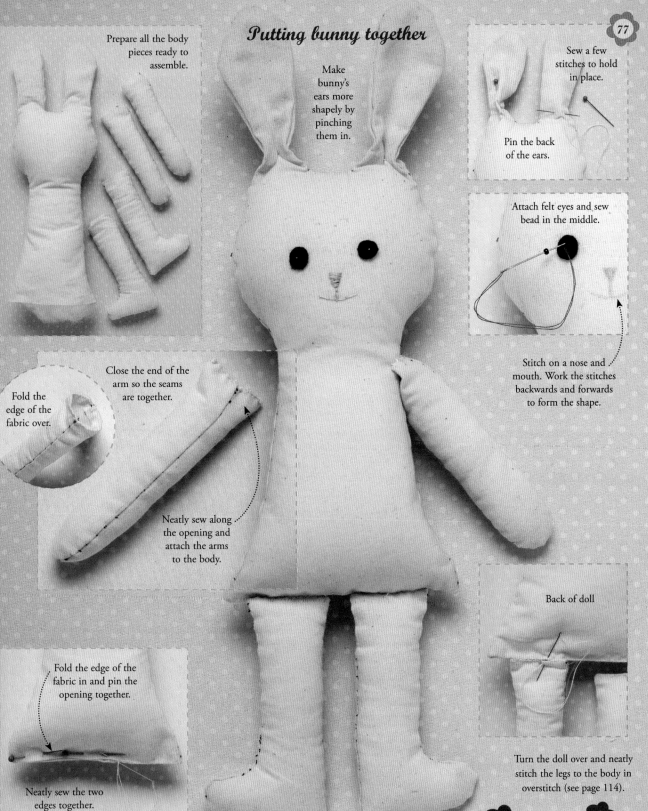

Prepare all the body pieces ready to assemble.

Make bunny's ears more shapely by pinching them in.

Sew a few stitches to hold in place.

Pin the back of the ears.

Attach felt eyes and sew bead in the middle.

Stitch on a nose and mouth. Work the stitches backwards and forwards to form the shape.

Fold the edge of the fabric over.

Close the end of the arm so the seams are together.

Neatly sew along the opening and attach the arms to the body.

Back of doll

Fold the edge of the fabric in and pin the opening together.

Neatly sew the two edges together.

Turn the doll over and neatly stitch the legs to the body in overstitch (see page 114).

For the dress and bag

You will need

- Colourful cotton fabric, two pieces 15cm x 15cm (6in x 6in)
- Matching fabric for headscarf
- Sewing kit (see page 112) • Felt, two pieces 6cm x 6cm (2½in x 2½in)
- Felt scraps for eyes and motifs
- Ribbons

Handy tip

Use pinking shears (see page 113) to cut out the dress. This gives the fabric pretty edges, and won't need finishing.

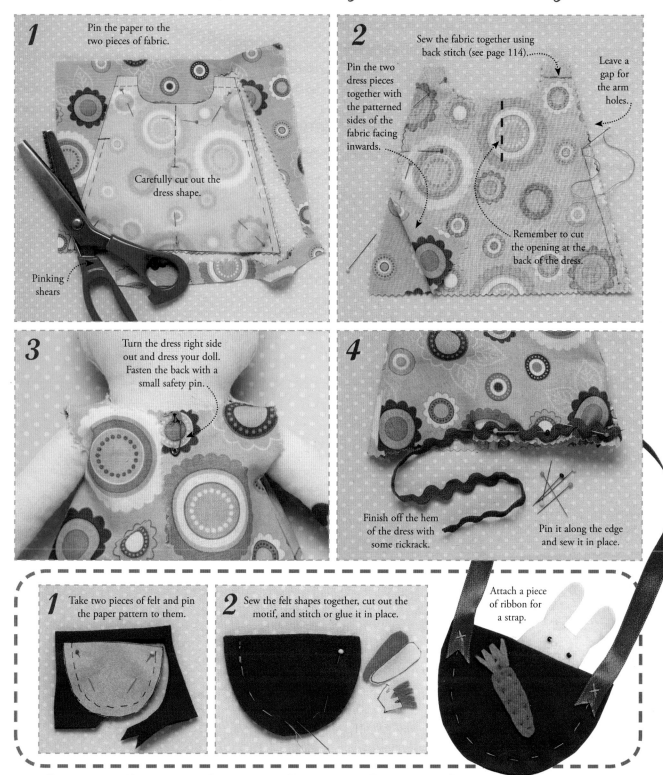

1 Pin the paper to the two pieces of fabric.

Carefully cut out the dress shape.

Pinking shears

2 Sew the fabric together using back stitch (see page 114).

Pin the two dress pieces together with the patterned sides of the fabric facing inwards.

Leave a gap for the arm holes.

Remember to cut the opening at the back of the dress.

3 Turn the dress right side out and dress your doll. Fasten the back with a small safety pin.

4 Finish off the hem of the dress with some rickrack.

Pin it along the edge and sew it in place.

1 Take two pieces of felt and pin the paper pattern to them.

2 Sew the felt shapes together, cut out the motif, and stitch or glue it in place.

Attach a piece of ribbon for a strap.

Doodlephants

Who can resist a doodle?

This project combines a soft toy and a doodled design inspired by the medallions and flowers used on Indian fabrics. First make a plain elephant then doodle away.

Draw out your design directly on to the fabric.

Use felt for the ears and tail.

Permanent markers

Pens to use

You don't need special fabric pens for this project. Permanent markers will work just as well.

Cut the end of the tail into thin strips.

Calico or pale-coloured cotton fabric will show up your doodles really well.

You will need

Cotton fabric such as calico for elephant body 60cm x 25cm (24in x 10in) • Grey felt for tail and ears • Sewing kit (see page 112) • Permanent marker pens • Soft toy filling • Buttons for eyes

How to make an elephant

Follow the steps on page 82.

1

Fill the area with your design, leaving spaces that can be coloured in.

2

Now colour in your design.

3 Finished colouring?

The great thing about doodling is that the design is endless. There's always a little space that you can fill with a dot or a swirl.

Complete both sides of your elephant.

Find the pattern for Doodlephants on page 84.

Make a plain elephant

1 Pin the template to two pieces of fabric and cut out the body shapes.

2 Pin the two pieces together.

Use backstitch (see page 114) to join the pieces. Leave an opening for the filling.

Stitch about 5mm (¼in) from the edge.

3 Turn the elephant inside out.

Fill the elephant so it is soft but firm. Stitch up the opening.

4 Ears

Tail

Felt size 10cm x 2cm (4in x 1in). Fold the tail piece in half and stitch together.

Felt size 20cm x 8cm (8in x 3in). Cut out the piece of felt for the ears.

5 Lay the felt ears over the top of the elephant.

Stitch in place along the centre.

6 Stitch the tail in place at the back, across the seam.

Cut the end of the tail to give a fringe effect.

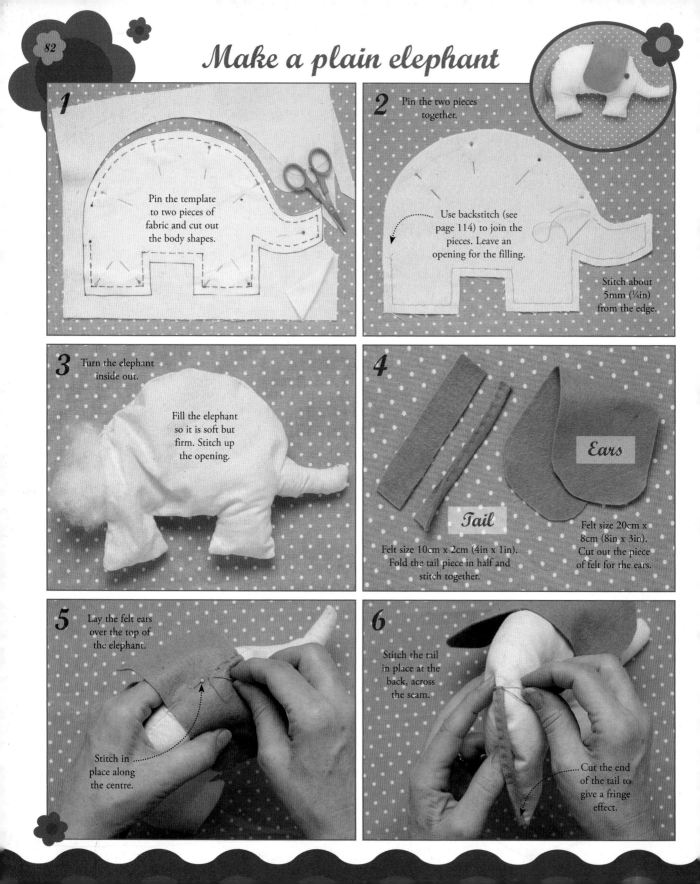

Cotton fabric

These elephants are made out of cotton calico. This is a cheap and versatile fabric. If you can't get hold of it try a plain pale-coloured cotton fabric.

Opening

Stitch up to these dots to leave
an opening for filling the toy.

Fold

Doodlephant tail

Doodlephant

How to make...

A PAPER PATTERN FROM
THIS TEMPLATE

Lay tracing paper over the page and trace
out the lines. Cut around the shape and
pin the paper pattern to your fabric. See
page 40 for more details.

After sewing the two
shapes together snip along
these lines – it will help
with shaping the fabric.

Dotted line

Stitch along this line.

Solid line

Cut the fabric out
along this line.

Doodlephant ears

Double thickness fabric.

Fold line of the fabric.

Fabric elephants Not just for doodling – these elephants look good in colourful cotton fabric too.

Jumbo-sized elephants

Scan the template page from the book, increase the size to 200 per cent. Print it out and attach the paper copy to your fabric. Make up the elephant as shown for the Doodlephant.

This elephant is made at 200 per cent.

Your little pony

Full of swishing tails and manes, this project will take you back to your childhood. You can have endless fun creating a stable full of little ponies.

You will need

- Cotton fabric 2 pieces 20cm x 20cm (8in x 8in)
- Knitting yarn
- Tapestry needle
- Soft toy stuffing
- Felt and buttons
- Sewing kit (see page 112)

The mane is made from lengths of yarn 15cm (6in) long sewn through the fabric to form a small tassel.

To make the tail

To make the swishy tail, cut 10 lengths of yarn 24cm (10in) long. Knot them together in the middle – a slip knot works well, (see page 116).

Make a mouth using backstitch (see page 114).

Finish off the eye with a button stitched over the eyelash.

Once the tail is in place, cut the yarn to the same length.

Find the pattern

for your little pony on page 88.

How to make your pony

1 Pin the paper to two pieces of fabric and carefully cut out the shape.

2 Make sure the patterned sides of the fabric face each other.

Leave an opening at the top to allow for filling.

Sew around the shape 5mm (¼in) from the edge using backstitch.

Turn the shape right side out and fill. Work the filling in to all the corners and use slipstitch (see page 114) to close the opening.

How to attach the mane

Insert the needle from the left and pull the yarn through but not all the way. Then insert the needle from the right and pull the yarn through to leave a loop.

Take the needle off the thread and adjust thread so ends are equal.

Stitch the tail to the pony.

Sew the ears either side of the head, and apply the eyes in the same way.

Thread the ends of the yarn through the loop and pull.

Your little pony

'V' shapes

After sewing the two shapes together snip along these lines – it will help with shaping the fabric.

Dotted line

Stitch along this line.

Solid line

Cut the fabric out along this line.

Ear

Opening

Stitch up to these dots to leave an opening for filling the toy.

Your other ponies

Use your pony template to make a whole stable full. Have a go experimenting with different patterned cotton fabric.

Jolly the Giraffe

Jolly and Jill the giraffes are standing tall — they can easily stand up for themselves with this simple design, and require no complicated shaping.

Lovely legs

For your giraffe, choose some fun fabric like Jolly's, which looks very giraffe-like. For an extra special effect use a contrasting fabric for the inside of your giraffe's legs.

You will need

- Cotton fabric 2 pieces 30cm x 30cm (12in x 12in) for the main body colour and 20cm x 24cm (8in x 9½in) contrasting colour for the inside of the legs
- Buttons for eyes and to attach the legs • Felt for tails and ears
- Soft toy filling • Sewing kit (see page 112)

Find the pattern

for Jolly the Giraffe on page 94

How to make a giraffe

1

Fold the fabric for the inside legs and cut two to make four pieces altogether.

For the body, take two pieces of fabric and lay them with the pattern facing inwards. Cut out the shape using a traced version of the template (see page 94).

For the outside legs, cut two double-layered fabric pieces, for a total of four fabric pieces.

2

Use backstitch (see page 114) to stitch all round the legs.

Leave an opening at the top.

Place the inside and outside leg together.

Leave an opening at the base of the body.

3

Turn the body and leg pieces right side out, so the pattern is on the outside.

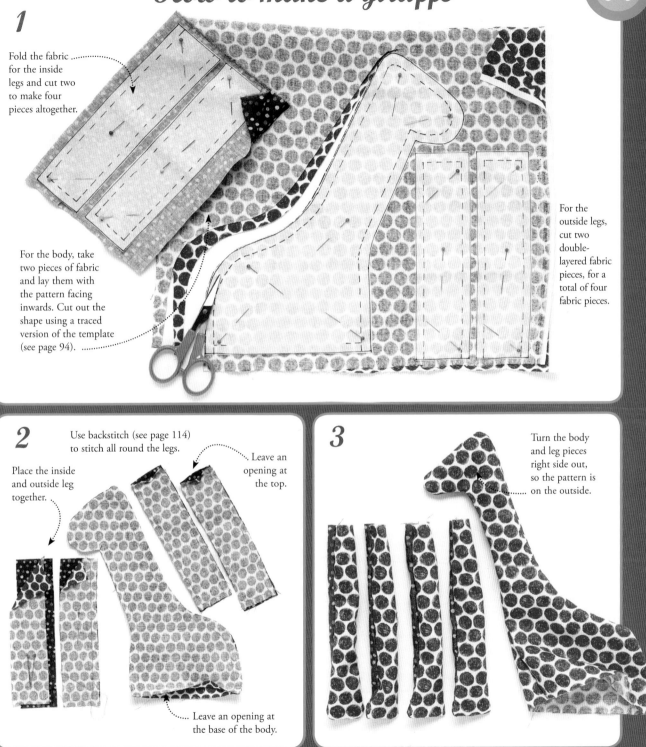

4

Fill all the body parts so they are soft but firm.

Work the stuffing evenly into the head and neck.

5

To finish off the legs, neatly fold the top of the fabric over and pin the openings together.

Neatly sew up the openings in slipstitch (see page 114).

6

Fold in the edges of the fabric and stitch up the opening using slipstitch.

Giraffes on the move

Because the legs are stitched on to the body separately they will move independently. This means you can put your giraffe into all sort of poses.

How to put the pieces together

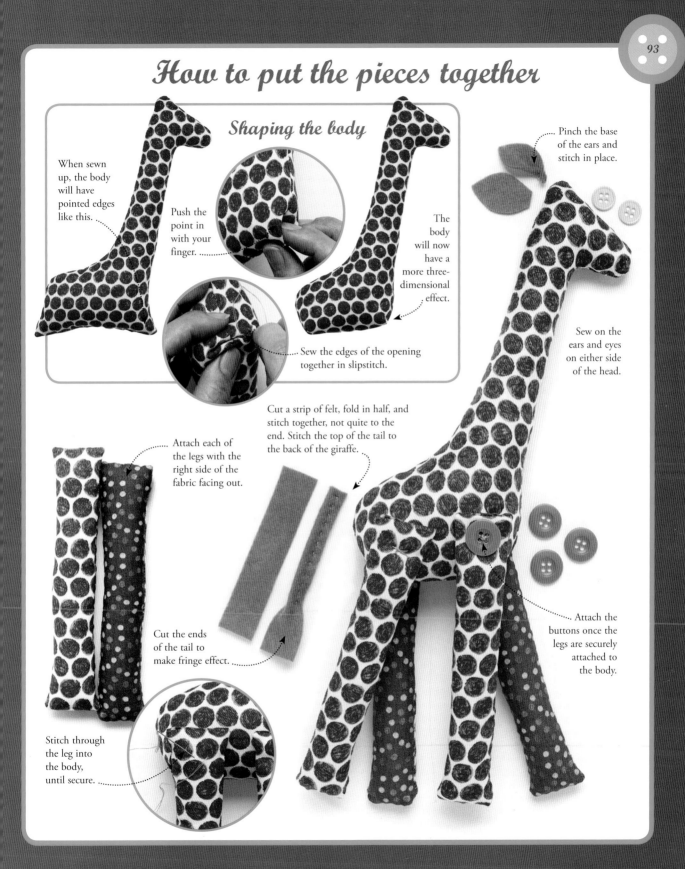

Shaping the body

When sewn up, the body will have pointed edges like this.

Push the point in with your finger.

The body will now have a more three-dimensional effect.

Sew the edges of the opening together in slipstitch.

Pinch the base of the ears and stitch in place.

Sew on the ears and eyes on either side of the head.

Attach each of the legs with the right side of the fabric facing out.

Cut a strip of felt, fold in half, and stitch together, not quite to the end. Stitch the top of the tail to the back of the giraffe.

Cut the ends of the tail to make fringe effect.

Stitch through the leg into the body, until secure.

Attach the buttons once the legs are securely attached to the body.

Jolly the Giraffe

Dotted line
Stitch along this line

Solid line
Cut fabric out along
this line.

How to make...
A PAPER PATTERN FROM
THIS TEMPLATE
Lay tracing paper over the page
and trace the lines. Cut
around the shape and pin
the paper pattern to your
fabric. See page 40 for
more details.

Giraffe legs x 4
Double-thickness fabric

Fold fabric on this line

Tail

Ear

Fold along the
line to shape
the ear.

Opening
● Stitch up to these dots to leave an opening for filling the toy. ●

You can make small ones too.

Standing tall

Try making different-sized giraffes. Simply scan the template page, increase the size by 150 per cent, print it out, and make up the giraffe as shown in the steps.

Cat's bed

Make a comfy bed cover for a sleepy toy. This patchwork of squares made from two different fabrics is one of the easiest designs to put together.

You will need

- 2 pieces of contrasting fabric
- Paper • Felt for backing
- Sewing kit (see page 112)
- Ribbon for decoration

How to put the patches together

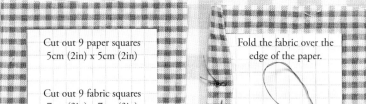

Cut out 9 paper squares 5cm (2in) x 5cm (2in)

Cut out 9 fabric squares 7cm (3in) x 7cm (3in) 5 squares of one fabric and 4 of the other.

1 ⋯ Place the paper in the centre of the fabric.

Fold the fabric over the edge of the paper.

2 ⋯ Sew the fabric to the paper using large stitches.

3 Stitch all the way around.

Sew the squares together.

Make the stitches small and neat.

Undo the tacking stitch and remove the paper.

Cut the felt to the same size as the sewn patches.

Make the most of the fabric designs by putting them in the centre of the patch.

⋯ Carefully stitch the felt to the patches using running stitch (see page 114).

Zzzzz....

Zzzz....

Handy tip

Try adjusting the size of your quilt. Either make more small square patches or simply make larger squares. It can be as big as you want, depending on the size of your cat.

4
Animals in stitches

Pictures in stitches

Big and small. You can make the same picture in a different size by using a different thread-count fabric.

You will need
- 8-count and 14-count cross stitch fabric
- Sewing kit (see page 112)

Make a picture

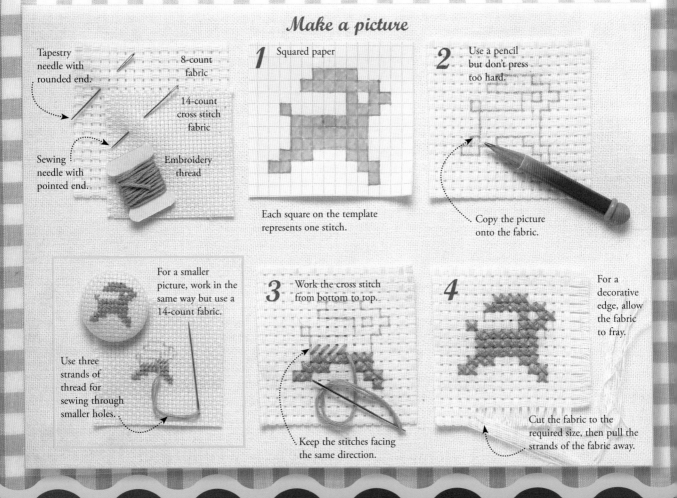

Tapestry needle with rounded end.

8-count fabric

14-count cross stitch fabric

Sewing needle with pointed end.

Embroidery thread

1 Squared paper

Each square on the template represents one stitch.

2 Use a pencil but don't press too hard.

Copy the picture onto the fabric.

For a smaller picture, work in the same way but use a 14-count fabric.

Use three strands of thread for sewing through smaller holes.

3 Work the cross stitch from bottom to top.

Keep the stitches facing the same direction.

4 For a decorative edge, allow the fabric to fray.

Cut the fabric to the required size, then pull the strands of the fabric away.

See page 102
for templates

Glue your pictures
to the front of
greeting cards.

DIY key
fob from
craft shop

There are lots of ways you can use
your pictures – from greeting cards
and buttons, to box lids and key
fobs. They are just perfect as gifts.

Customize your stuff
by attaching different-
sized pictures to your
belongings. Create a
matching set instantly!

Animal patterns

Every square equals a stitch.

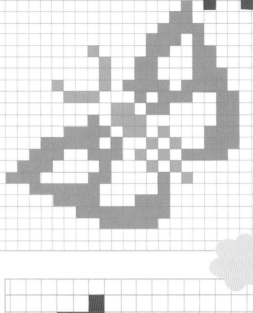

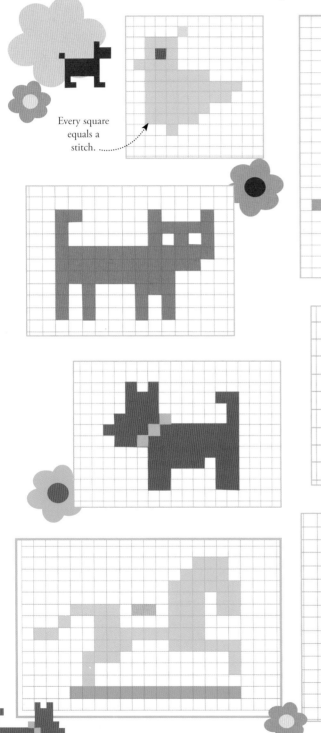

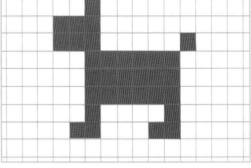

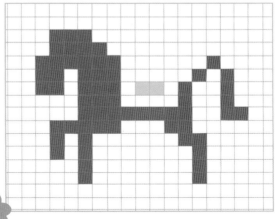

Fill in the gaps between the animals with cross stitch patterns.

These hoops make perfect picture frames for your work. Just fold the fabric behind the frame when you have finished sewing.

The bigger picture

To design your big picture it helps to plan it out first on squared paper. Then take a piece of 8-count fabric larger than the area of your design. Count out the squares on the fabric and begin stitching. When complete, cut around your work and fray the edge to make an attractive border.

Follow the pattern

Centre the design on the canvas and use the coloured squares to position the stitches and match the colours. Begin stitching the main part of the image first, then work the other colours one at a time.

You will need

A piece of canvas 10cm x 13cm (4in x 5in)

Selection of tapestry wool and needle.

Felt pens

Pet portraits

Draw a picture of your favourite pet. With some pens and squared paper turn the portrait into coloured squares. No pets? No problem: stitch this little cat instead. Just choose different-coloured wool if you want to change the colour of the cat and background.

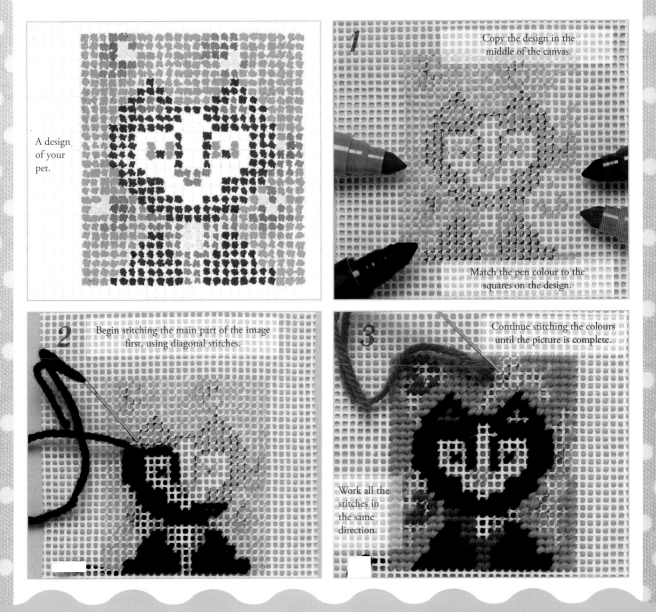

A design of your pet.

1 Copy the design in the middle of the canvas.

Match the pen colour to the squares on the design.

2 Begin stitching the main part of the image first, using diagonal stitches.

3 Continue stitching the colours until the picture is complete.

Work all the stitches in the same direction.

Stitch a doodle

Next time you're doodling why not transform the designs into stitches?
Select your scribble, copy it directly onto the fabric, and stitch away.

You will need

- Your doodles • Embroidery hoop
- Cotton or linen fabric • Embroidery threads • Sewing kit (see page 112)
- Pencil

Transfer your design onto the fabric with a pencil.

NOTE: for a bag, place the hoop in the centre of the fabric.

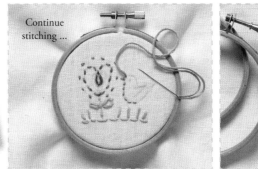

Stitch over the lines.

Continue stitching ...

Remove the hoop.

How to make a bag

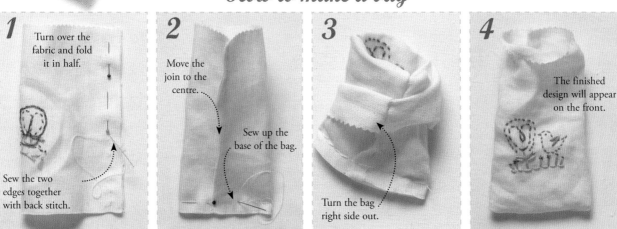

1 Turn over the fabric and fold it in half.

Sew the two edges together with back stitch.

2 Move the join to the centre.

Sew up the base of the bag.

3 Turn the bag right side out.

4 The finished design will appear on the front.

Running stitch

Single chain stitch

Garden bird

Doodles make great buttons.

Use a running stitch to follow the outline of your doodle.

Add colour to your doodles by using coloured thread.

Doodle decorations

Make your doodles work. Here's a project that combines doodling with something useful – a decorated sewing case for your needles and threads.

You will need

- Felt 32cm x 11cm (12½in x 4¼in)
- Cotton fabric 16cm x 9½cm (6¼in x 3½in)
- Embroidery thread
- Sewing kit (see page 112)
- Felt scraps to make motifs

Fold the felt in half to find the centre line. To make the flaps, measure 7cm (2¾in) from each side. Fold over and crease.

1

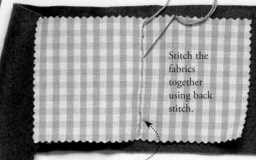

Stitch the fabrics together using back stitch.

Place the cotton fabric in the centre of the felt.

Flap 7cm (2¾in) wide

2

Place the felt motif on the front of the wallet and stitch it in position.

3

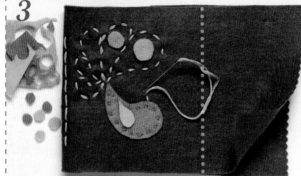

Build up your design with stitched outlines, such as the bird's tail.

Fill in the outlines with felt shapes and more stitches.

4

To make the side pocket, fold over the flap and pin it in position under the cotton fabric.

Fold the flap over and pin in position.

5

Sew across the top and bottom edges of the wallet.

Exotic bird design

Just like a doodle with pen and paper, this design is made with fabric and thread. Begin your design with a felt shape such as this bird, then play with the stitching, making shapes and filling the spaces. There's no need to draw it out first – just see where the design takes you.

Handy pockets to stow away your threads.

5

Sewing kit
and
useful know-how

Creating creatures

All the projects in this book will begin by telling you what materials you'll need to make it. The most essential piece of equipment is the Sewing kit – have this ready at all times. Also, shown here are other things that you'll find useful.

Sewing kit

Here are the sewing essentials – keep them collected up in a handy box.

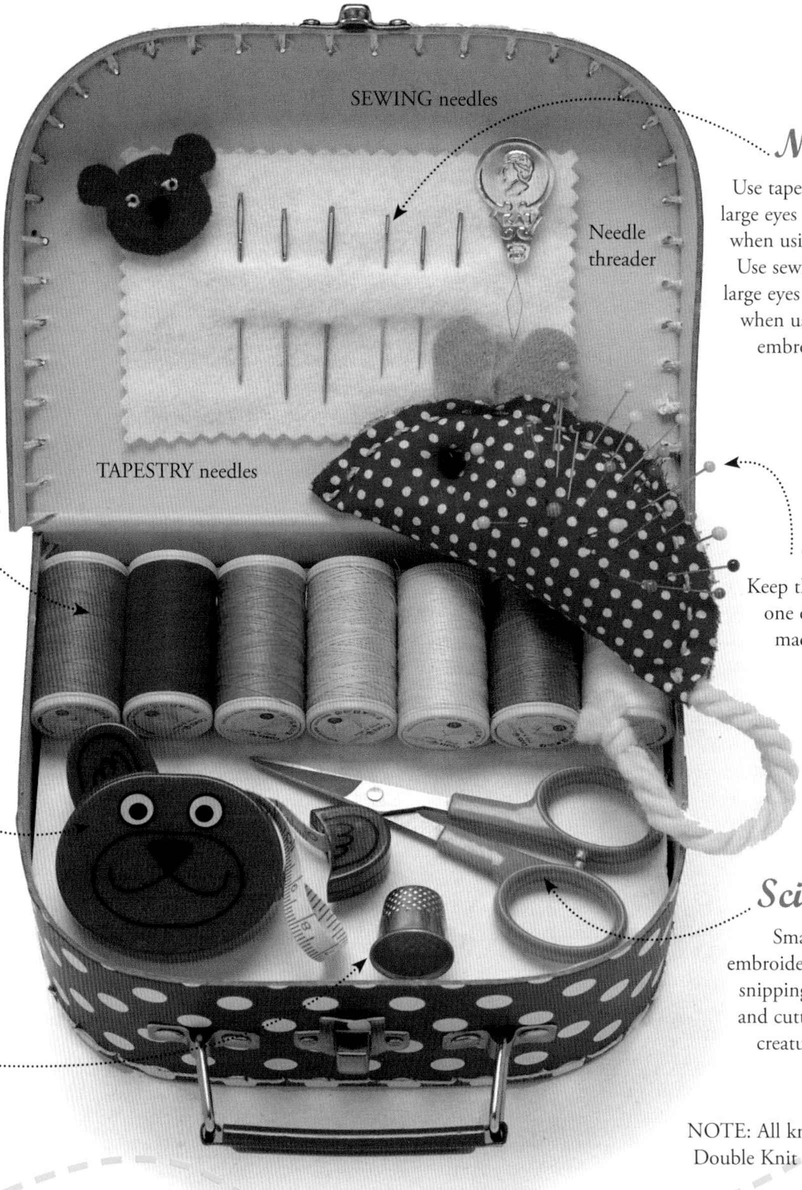

Sewing thread

Keep an array of threads plus some other creature colours such as black, grey, and brown.

Tape measure

For measuring up your fabric when starting a project and some precise positioning.

Thimble

On big projects doing a lot of hand stitching can make your middle finger sore – use the thimble on your middle finger to push the needle through.

SEWING needles

TAPESTRY needles

Needle threader

Needles

Use tapestry needles with large eyes and rounded ends when using knitting yarn. Use sewing needles with large eyes and pointed ends when using sewing and embroidery thread.

Pins

Keep them to hand in one of your home made cushions.

Scissors

Small sharp embroidery scissors for snipping off threads and cutting out tiny creature shapes.

NOTE: All knitting patterns use Double Knit (DK) weight yarn

These will be useful too...

From cutting out larger pieces of fabric to stuffing your projects.

Large scissors

For cutting out templates and larger pieces of fabric these large scissors are best. It helps if the scissors are sharp as this makes them easier to use and they give better results.

Embroidery thread

The thickness of this thread is good when you want to see the stitches. It is used for decorative stitches as well.

Felt fabric

Felt is so versatile – it's easy to shape and it doesn't fray when cut. This makes it perfect to use for tiny projects and great creature features.

Pinking shears

These scissors will prevent cotton fabric fraying because their blade is zig-zag shaped. The effect is attractive as well and can be used for decoration.

Soft toy filling

This polyester fibre is used for all the projects in this book. It's very soft and can be easily worked into all the different animal shapes.

Buttons

Colourful buttons in all sizes are good for eyes and noses, and make great decorations.

How to stitch

Here are the stitches that are used for the projects. They all have a different job to do when you are joining fabric together for cushions, bags, and patchwork pieces.

How to start and finish

Begin stitching with a knot at the end of the thread. To end a row of stitches, make a tiny stitch, but do not pull it tight. Bring the thread back up through the loop and pull tight. Do this once more in the same spot, then cut the thread.

Running stitch

This is a very versatile stitch used for seams, joining fabric together, and gathering.

Keep the stitches and the spaces between them small and even.

Backstitch

This is the strongest stitch. It makes a continuous line of stitches so it is best for joining two pieces of fabric securely, such as the sides of a bag.

Make the stitch then bring the needle back to the place where the last stitch is finished.

VIEW FROM REVERSE

Bring the needle out ready to begin the next stitch.

Tacking stitch

This is a temporary stitch. It will be removed but it is useful for holding pieces of fabric in place before you sew them together properly. It is also known as a basting stitch.

Tacking stitches are like running stitches but are larger and don't need to be even.

Overstitch

These are tiny, neat, and even stitches that are almost invisible. Use them to top sew two finished edges together, such as when you are joining patchwork pieces.

Insert the needle diagonally from the back of the fabric.

Pick up only two or three threads of fabric.

Slip stitch

Use slip stitch when you want the stitches to be invisible. This stitch is made by slipping the thread under a fold of fabric. It is often used to join two folded edges, such as the openings of cushions.

Slide the needle into the fold of the fabric.

Bring the needle out then slide the needle in the other side.

Lazy daisy stitch

This pretty stitch is very useful for embroidery decoration. Draw out your daisy design first in light pencil, then follow the lines with your stitches.

1 Tie a knot in your thread and pull it up through the beginning of a petal and down at the end.

2 Now bring it up through another petal until you have finished the flower.

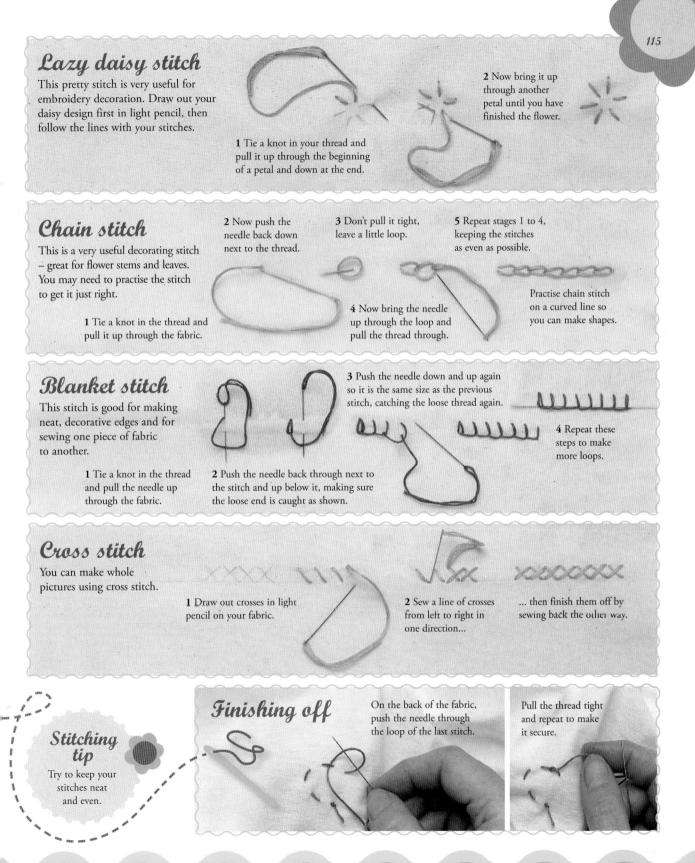

Chain stitch

This is a very useful decorating stitch – great for flower stems and leaves. You may need to practise the stitch to get it just right.

1 Tie a knot in the thread and pull it up through the fabric.

2 Now push the needle back down next to the thread.

3 Don't pull it tight, leave a little loop.

4 Now bring the needle up through the loop and pull the thread through.

5 Repeat stages 1 to 4, keeping the stitches as even as possible.

Practise chain stitch on a curved line so you can make shapes.

Blanket stitch

This stitch is good for making neat, decorative edges and for sewing one piece of fabric to another.

1 Tie a knot in the thread and pull the needle up through the fabric.

2 Push the needle back through next to the stitch and up below it, making sure the loose end is caught as shown.

3 Push the needle down and up again so it is the same size as the previous stitch, catching the loose thread again.

4 Repeat these steps to make more loops.

Cross stitch

You can make whole pictures using cross stitch.

1 Draw out crosses in light pencil on your fabric.

2 Sew a line of crosses from left to right in one direction...

... then finish them off by sewing back the other way.

Finishing off

On the back of the fabric, push the needle through the loop of the last stitch.

Pull the thread tight and repeat to make it secure.

Stitching tip

Try to keep your stitches neat and even.

Loops called stitches

Rows

Ball of yarn

How to knit

From casting on to casting off — whether you are just learning or already have the knitting know-how, these pages are a handy reference.

Slip knot:
The first stitch on the needle is knotted so the yarn stays on.

Pull the ends of the yarn tight – now you have the first stitch.

Take a ball of yarn and make a loop at the end.

Bring the yarn through the loop to create a new loop.

Keep pulling the new loop through.

Attach the new loop to the needle.

Casting on:
There are many ways to cast on. This method uses the thumb.

Wrap the yarn around your thumb as shown.

Pick up the yarn with the needle.

Let the yarn go from your thumb onto the needle.

Continue doing this...

... until you have enough stitches.

Joining new yarn

Use this when adding a new ball of yarn or making stripes.

2 Slide the knot up the yarn to the needle.

1 Tie the new yarn to the old yarn with a loose knot.

3 Continue knitting as usual.

Knit in a new colour

Here the knitting is shown on the reverse side. Join the new yarn as shown (left). To tidy up the loose ends of both colours, gather them up with the working yarn as you knit.

How many?

The projects in this book tell you how many stitches to cast on. Lots of stitches give you a wide fabric, while few stitches make a narrow fabric.

When you are starting a new row, start with the first stitch on the right and work towards the left.

The yarn will be on the right as well.

Getting started

You will need to cast on the number of stitches required in the pattern. The stitches that are being worked will be on the left-hand needle, and the ones you have made will go on the right.

Casting off

1 Begin the row by knitting two stitches.

2 Pick up the first stitch with the left needle.

3 Carry this first stitch over the second stitch and over the end of the needle.

4 Repeat steps 1–3...

5 ... until one stitch remains. Open up the loop

6 Cut the yarn and place the end in the loop.

7 Pull the yarn to close the loop.

Tidy away ends

Sewing in ends when adding new yarn or tidying the loose ends of finished pieces.

Use this method when tidying joined yarn and when knitting stripes.

Use this method when tidying loose ends of finished pieces.

Thread the end with a tapestry needle.

Sew the thread into the edge of the knitting.

Bring the needle out and cut the yarn.

Thread the needle onto the loose end and sew down the side of the knitting.

Bring the needle out and cut the yarn.

Knit stitch

Also called plain stitch – this is the most useful stitch. It's simple to make, and used in most projects – it's used to make Ted!

Method 1

1 Hold the knitting with your hands in this position.

Take the yarn around the back.

Place the needle in the back of the stitch.

2 Wrap the yarn under and around the needle from right to left.

Method 2 This method might be helpful for left-handers.

1 Place the yarn between the fingers of your left hand.

2 Use your index finger to move the yarn.

Place the needle into the stitch.

Garter stitch

Garter stitch isn't an actual stitch but the name given to a piece of knitting where every row is knitted in knit stitch. The effect is bobbly on both sides.

Garter stitch is also made if you knit every row in purl stitch.

3 Pull on the yarn and move the needle from the back to the front.

4 The right needle is now on top of the left one and has taken the stitch with it.

5 Slide the top needle to the right. The stitch will now be transferred onto the right needle, completing the stitch.

Begin the next stitch as in step 1.

3 Bring the yarn under and over the needle.

4 Bring the needle with the loop of yarn to the front.

5 Take the needle with the stitch off the left hand needle.

Begin the next stitch as in step 1.

For purl stitch, the needle goes in the front of the stitch.

The yarn also goes at the front too.

Purl stitch

Working from the front — This stitch is made by the needle going in the front of the stitch. It's when knit and purl stitch rows are alternated that the knitting looks smooth – just like the Knittens!

Method 1

1 Hold the knitting with your hands in this position.

Bring the yarn to the front.

Place the needle in the front of the stitch.

2 Take the yarn between the needles.

3 Wrap it round the needle from right to left.

Method 2 This method might be helpful for left-handers.

1 Place the right hand needle in the front of the stitch.

Hold the knitting in your left hand with the yarn at the front of the work.

2 Wind the yarn around the front of the needle.

3 Wind the yarn around again.

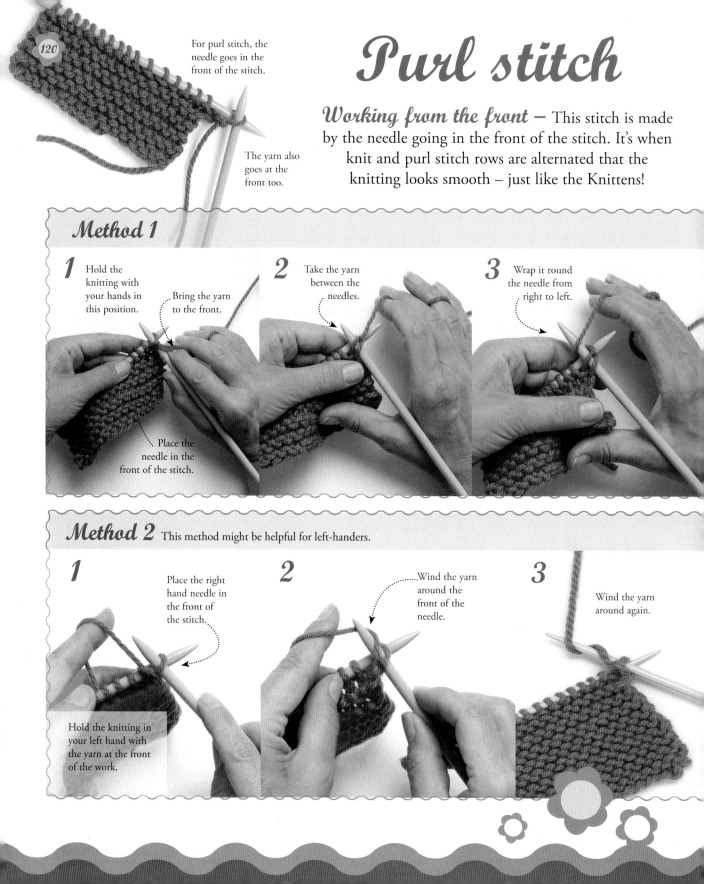

Purl stitch + Knit stitch = Stocking stitch

Stocking stitch isn't an actual stitch at all. Instead it is made by working a knit row then a purl row, a knit row then a purl row and so on. The result is a smooth front to the knitting and a "bobbly" back.

BACK
The purl-stitch side

FRONT
The knit-stitch side

4 Pull on the yarn and move the needle from front to back ...

5 ... taking the stitch with it.

6 Take the rest of the yarn off the needle to complete the stitch.

Begin the next stitch as in step 1.

4 Bring the right hand needle from front to back taking the yarn with it.

5 Pull the rest of the stitch off the needle.

6 Now you are ready to begin the next stitch, starting at step 1 again.

Knitting shapes

INCREASE SHAPE

An extra stitch has been made at the beginning and the end of each row.

Two stitches have been knitted together at the beginning and end of each row.

DECREASE SHAPE

You can shape the knitting by adding (increasing) or taking away (decreasing) stitches. There are many different ways to do this, but here are two simple methods you can try.

Make a stitch – increasing

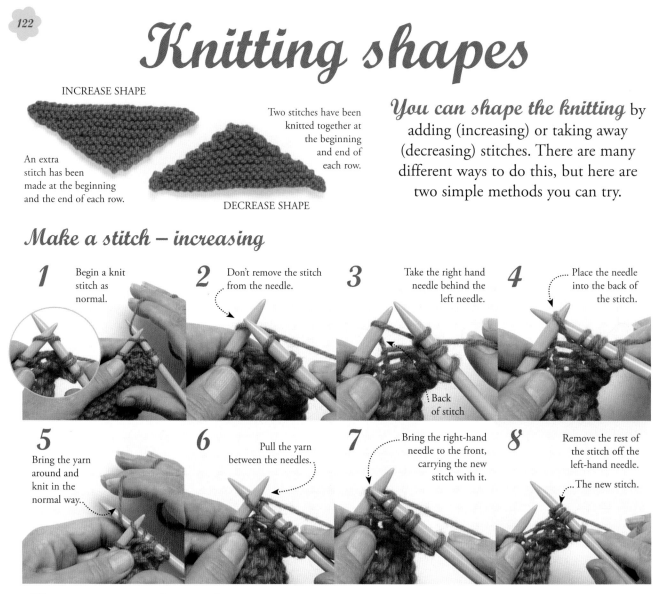

1 Begin a knit stitch as normal.

2 Don't remove the stitch from the needle.

3 Take the right hand needle behind the left needle.

4 Place the needle into the back of the stitch.

Back of stitch

5 Bring the yarn around and knit in the normal way.

6 Pull the yarn between the needles.

7 Bring the right-hand needle to the front, carrying the new stitch with it.

8 Remove the rest of the stitch off the left-hand needle.

The new stitch.

Knit two together – decreasing

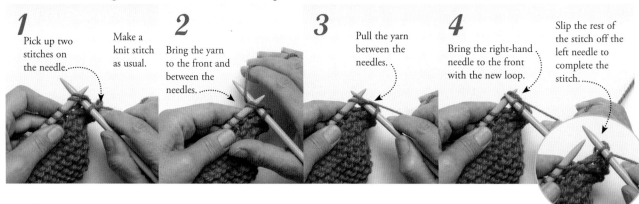

1 Pick up two stitches on the needle. Make a knit stitch as usual.

2 Bring the yarn to the front and between the needles.

3 Pull the yarn between the needles.

4 Bring the right-hand needle to the front with the new loop.

Slip the rest of the stitch off the left needle to complete the stitch.

Threading needles

NEEDLE TYPES

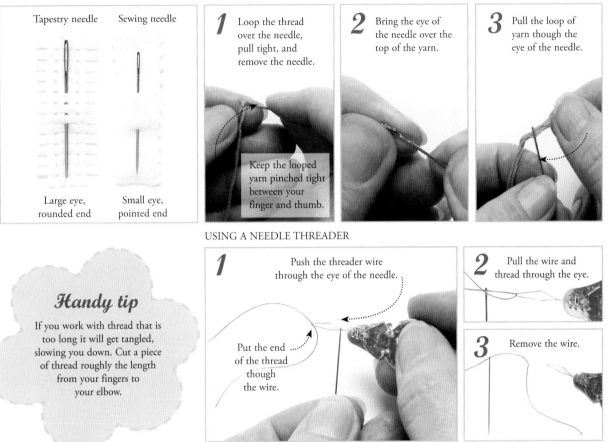

| Tapestry needle | Sewing needle |
| Large eye, rounded end | Small eye, pointed end |

THREADING EMBROIDERY THREAD OR WOOLLEN YARN

1 Loop the thread over the needle, pull tight, and remove the needle.

Keep the looped yarn pinched tight between your finger and thumb.

2 Bring the eye of the needle over the top of the yarn.

3 Pull the loop of yarn though the eye of the needle.

USING A NEEDLE THREADER

1 Push the threader wire through the eye of the needle.

Put the end of the thread though the wire.

2 Pull the wire and thread through the eye.

3 Remove the wire.

Handy tip

If you work with thread that is too long it will get tangled, slowing you down. Cut a piece of thread roughly the length from your fingers to your elbow.

Sewing on a button

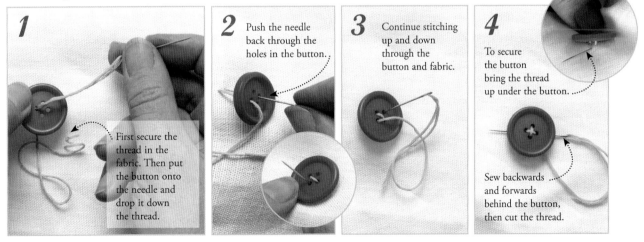

1 First secure the thread in the fabric. Then put the button onto the needle and drop it down the thread.

2 Push the needle back through the holes in the button.

3 Continue stitching up and down through the button and fabric.

4 To secure the button bring the thread up under the button.

Sew backwards and forwards behind the button, then cut the thread.

Index